SOCIAL SECURITY

Christina Masciotti

BROADWAY PLAY PUBLISHING INC
224 E 62nd St, NY, NY 10065
www.broadwayplaypub.com
info@broadwayplaypub.com

SOCIAL SECURITY

© Copyright 2017 Christina Masciotti

Cover photo by Maria Baranova

First edition: September 2017
I S B N: 978-0-88145-733-9

Book design: Marie Donovan
Page make-up: Adobe InDesign
Typeface: Palatino

SOCIAL SECURITY was first produced at The Bushwick Starr (Jennifer Conley Darling and Eva C Scanlan, Producers) opening on 25 February 2015. The cast and creative contributors were:

JUNE .... Elizabeth Dement
SISSY... Cynthia Hopkins
WAYNE .... T Ryder Smith

Director..Paul Lazar
Stage manager...Derek Spaldo
Set ....Sara C Walsh
Lights .... Simon Harding
Costumes..Jacob A Climer
Sound .... Ben Williams
Production associate .... James Zebooker

CHARACTERS

JUNE, *in her late seventies or early eighties. She is a retired pretzel factory worker, deaf from forty years with machines. A seventh grade drop-out, her development is stunted, and she seems to be going through life as a wide-eyed, seventh grader, remarkably childlike, blissfully ignorant, and incredibly trusting. She can't hear herself, so she speaks louder than normal, but otherwise her speech reveals nothing of her deafness. Her deep Pennsylvania Dutch roots are apparent in the regional quirks of her voice. Desperate for company, she seems to speak non-stop at times, and no matter how grim her news may be, her chipper personality shines through. Her basic lip-reading skills are not up to par for conversations of any length, so she is forced to rely on hand-written notes from others. But when she wishes to avoid undesirable information, she is deft at ignoring what's been jotted down, and redirecting the discussion.*
She wears glasses, a gold watch, and a wardrobe from K-Mart, including Cuddler brand white, lace-up shoes.

WAYNE, *JUNE's landlord, in his mid-forties. He lives in the row-home next door to her. Once a successful podiatrist with a practice in his home, he is now on probation after a year in jail for substance abuse and identity theft. He is never without a steel travel mug.*

SISSY, *a neighbor, in her mid-forties, about five houses down the block. A reputable massage therapist with a genuine interest in helping people. Originally from Greece, she takes pride in her appearance.*

SETTING

Three row-homes on the 1100 block of Perkiomen Avenue in Reading, Pennsylvania.

Scene 1

(The space is divided into three separate row-homes, with no walls, or boundaries of any kind between them. The homes are differentiated only by the flooring: blonde hardwood, battered linoleum, and trampled gray carpet. The stage right hardwood floor curiously continues up the stage right wall, just as the stage left carpeting continues to creep almost all the way to the ceiling. The back wall of the space is obscured by slats of a black fringe curtain that part as JUNE enters, muttering, setting props, and the scarce set pieces: a massage mat, a kitchen table, a doily-strewn recliner, a tray table with a faux-wood-paneled clock radio, and a folding chair enlivened by a bright tie-on cushion. Once the last element is placed, she parts the slats to momentarily expose SISSY; the slats swing as she releases them. She cautiously parts another section of the fringe and WAYNE peers out. As JUNE drops the slats this time, she disappears behind the curtain only to re-enter hot on the heels of SISSY who can't seem to escape her. JUNE delivers her first lines a little formally at first, as if giving a book report to her class.)

JUNE: Tom passed away last night.

SISSY: Oh, no.

JUNE: Well, he had cancer so bad. Four days in the hospital. They couldn't do nothing for him. Brought him home in a hospital bed. I was up with him all night. He died at home.

SISSY: Oh, June.

JUNE: Aye, my god. Aye-yaye-yaye. We were supposed to pick up our Easter eggs from Margaret today. She makes dark chocolate and milk chocolate. She makes 'em herself with peanut butter. She has two dozen waiting for us, and I can't drive, Tom drove, I have his car, but I don't drive.

SISSY: You want me to drive you? I'm working today.

(JUNE *failed to read* SISSY's *lips.*)

JUNE: The doctor wanted to take me. I still call him doctor. But I don't know how to take him. First he's all right, then he don't know what to do. I think he's doing drugs with his thermos again. He has milk in it, and a pill at the bottom. Sometimes he pretends he drinks soda. I caught him in a few lies already. Yay-yuh! Uh-huh. I don't wanna get in a car with him.

SISSY: *(Opening her Day-Timer; to herself)* I don't know if I can reschedule anyone.

JUNE: See, all my relations, they're too far away. In Pottsville yet. My niece, Cathy, she's a nurse, she wanted me to take care of my sister.

SISSY: What about after five?

JUNE: *(Not understanding)* I couldn't, she was totally disabled. She had M S. She couldn't walk.

(SISSY *starts to write in the margin.*)

JUNE: Cathy dropped her off at my place, picked her up the next day, and put her in a nursing home. She was mad about that, but I couldn't do it. I never saw my sister again. Her name was Joyce. I'm June.

(SISSY *shows* JUNE *the note.*)

JUNE: *(Reading)* Five? Oh, yay-yuh! Renninger's stays open till six. Five would be all right.

SISSY: *(Ushering her out)* I'll see you at five.

JUNE: N'wait. I can't hear the doorbell. Here are my keys. You can have those. They were Tom's. *(About key ring)* He loved Betty Boop.

Scene 2

(JUNE walks back to her grey carpet. WAYNE is sitting on the folding chair where he has been throughout the first scene, clutching his steel tumbler, and watching her. The clock radio is broadcasting a Reading Phillies baseball game. She takes off her shoes, and nearly jumps out of her skin when she sees him.)

JUNE: Aye, you scared me half to death! What the heck are you doing in here? This ain't no open house.

WAYNE: *(Admiring her hair)* Woooow.

JUNE: *(Fluffing her hair)* I know they got nice this time, shut-up. *(Walking to her rocking chair)* Look at this rug. It was bad enough with the hospital bed.

(WAYNE turns up the radio.)

JUNE: Those are footprints from the electric man. Went in the basement to read the meter. It's a dirt floor, you know that? He comes up and tracks dirt all over the apartment. That basement floor should be restored. He told me dirt basement's are illegal.

(There are small tablets with pens on JUNE's tray table. WAYNE writes on a pad, and hands her the note.)

JUNE: *(Reading)* "They're-not-illegal." Well, he's a meter man, he would know. *(She sits and notices the leash of WAYNE's dog, protruding from her offstage kitchen floor.)*

WAYNE: *(Pointing to the leash, and making a drinking gesture)*

JUNE: That dog. He's not getting any. I put water out, I step in it later. I don't have more biscuits neither. This place is a mess enough. He gets crumbs all over. I'm not buying biscuits no more, that's your dog, you need to feed him.

(The ball game ends. WAYNE *turns off the radio, and writes on the pad.)*

WAYNE: *(Handing* JUNE *the pad)* Put on your shoes. We're going for a walk.

JUNE: *(Glancing at the pad)* Now don't get radical with me. I just sat down here.

WAYNE: *(Writing)* Don't you want to get today's paper?

JUNE: *(Glancing at the pad)* I'll go down later.

WAYNE: *(Extending his hand with great charm)* Let's go together.

JUNE: *(Fluffing her hair)* I'm not holding your hand. People'll think I'm mixed up with you. If you try anything, I'm turning right around. *(She gets up and puts her shoes on.)*

WAYNE: C'mon, Spike!

Scene 3

(A few hours later, JUNE *is sitting up in her rocking recliner, asleep.* SISSY *enters, and touches her gently on the shoulder.* JUNE *wakes up like she was never asleep.)*

JUNE: *(Shouting)* Oh, Sissy. He's a crook! I seen it with my own eyes!

SISSY: Excuse me. I didn't hear you. You spoke so softly.

JUNE: Yeah, he stole from the box on the corner. I gave Wayne three quarters, and I seen him take two papers out. Yay-yuh! He put three quarters in, I give him those, that was for my paper. *(Illustrating the mechanics of the newspaper box with gestures)* He held it down, and took another paper out. Two papers for one. What a landlord. Ain't that awful?

SISSY: *(Nodding)* Wayne is very good at that. Anything illegal. He's double-U oh seven. With no money and no influence. *(Pointing to her watch)* Are you ready to go?

JUNE: *(Holding up a foot, with dented shoe)* Look, that dog smashed my shoe down and everything.

SISSY: Oh, it's The Twilight Show.

JUNE: He oughtta give that dog a bath. He stinks. I pity that dog. He shouldn't a took that dog. He can't even take care of him. *(Pause)* Go ahead, sit down a while.

(SISSY does not move.)

JUNE: I just cleaned my sink out and sprayed it with Lysol. I don't like that garbage disposal, it keeps on stopping. *(Pause)* Go ahead, rest a minute. You had a lotta people, ain't?

(SISSY does not move.)

SISSY: Some people and a lot of phone calls. Those guys keep calling: "Is this a massage parlor?" "Do I need to wear pants?" "Do you do table showers?" I signed a contract for a year on the yellow pages website, and now everyone thinks I'm a hooker. That damn ad. *(Pause)* I shouldn't talk. You can't hear me.

(JUNE hands SISSY an envelope from her tray table.)

JUNE: Look at that. I just got that gas bill for a hundred twenty-five dollars. That's too high: four hundred twenty rent, hundred twenty-five gas, electric, and phone, and I have to buy food yet. That's a lot for me to pay out. For this dump. The electric, he puts it in his name, and he throws it in with my bills. He expects me to pay his electric bill.

(SISSY sees JUNE's pad, picks it up, and writes.)

SISSY: *(Showing* JUNE *what she wrote)* Maybe he thought it was yours.

JUNE: *(Glancing at the pad)* No, he throws it in with mine, a long time!

SISSY: *(Writing)* Throw it back to his house!

(JUNE reads to herself and laughs.)

JUNE: Yes, it's a mess. They have a gas bill layin' out there. All it has on it is twenty dollars. With a note from the doctor: "Can you pay this, Bob? If you can't, let me know." If they can't even pay a little twenty dollar gas bill, they should get the heck out! They have money for beer. Make 'em pay more!

SISSY: We should go. They're gonna close.

JUNE: Checks are always layin out there for them. Yay-yuh! Bob and Valerie. He was in the service, Bob, he's a veteran, not her. He has good veteran's checks. She's gettin veteran's checks, too, like he gets. I don't know how a woman gets that. They're not even married.

(SISSY nods trying to calm JUNE down. It has the opposite effect.)

JUNE: I never seen her pick up a broom! Or sweep the pavement. I may be nosy, but I ain't lazy!

(SISSY walks toward the door. JUNE follows.)

JUNE: You have to watch—they listen at the top of the steps to everything you say. *(Quieter)* You shoulda been here when those guys at the store knocked Bob on his rear end. He parked his car out here. Guys were movin, they had their red and blue movin trucks, and he pulls his car right in the middle. They told him to move it, he didn't want to, he was bringin a case of beer in, he got smart and yelled somethin to 'em, guy came out: *(Punch)* Boom. On his rear end. Just about like this. *(Punch)* Boom. Bob went down. Jesus mighty, aye my god. He flew down on the pavement. I was clappin when he got knocked down. And see how coward he is, he goes upstairs and sends Val down to yell at the guy. He sent her down, I saw her walk past the winda. *(Gesturing with both arms, a rotund figure)* He's supposed to be a hero. They're grouchy things. Valerie, she thinks she owns the whole place, the bitch. *(Looking)* Where's your car?

SISSY: *(Pointing)* Down there.

JUNE: *(Her head follows a truck driving past)* There's that ups! That's full of drugs for Wayne.

SISSY: Up's? Upstairs?

JUNE: There was a little brown one that stopped for him the other day. That's where he gets his pills. I told you I caught him the other day— *(Imitating signing)* He signed the paper. He got a package. I opened the door, and waved at the guy when he drove. *(She wags a no-no finger.)*

SISSY: *(Understanding that JUNE means: U P S)* June, that's his job. He needs to deliver the box.

JUNE: He don't know what he's delivering. He, he, he.

Scene 4

(JUNE and SISSY walk toward the black slats where groceries emerge on cue. A can of beans pops out.)

JUNE: Goya beans? *(Loud)* No, that's Spanish!

SISSY: *(Embarrassed)* Shh!

(A box of frozen Salisbury steaks presents itself; JUNE grabs it.)

JUNE: Those Salisbury steaks are delicious. What was I callin em? Sirloin patties. Look at my hair. They look terrible. I have to get my hair cut.

SISSY: I'm not taking you. Life is too soon. Too sure.
Too short.

(A white box of chocolates is extended. JUNE *takes it with
relish.)*

JUNE: Boy, are these good! Want one? Here. They're
real good. Try.

*(*SISSY *reluctantly selects an egg from the box: it's sloppily
covered with chocolate and has bald spots of peanut butter.
She puts it in her mouth, and grimaces.)*

JUNE: *(Handing the box to* SISSY*)* Take the whole box.
Tommy ordered those. I like milk chocolate better
anyway.

(A bright bag of cookies pops out. JUNE *hesitates.)*

JUNE: Cookies. I better not. Doctors told me bananas,
apples, and toast until that cholesterol comes down.
He said there's different things I can't eat. I don't know
what to do with myself. Sometimes I don't even have
an appetite. Tommy's gone.

SISSY: *(Writing one word on a coupon: bananas)* Should I
get you some bananas?

(Bananas loom between them.)

JUNE: My foot needs work. I think that big toenail
might have to come off. I need to go to the foot doctor.

SISSY: Go.

JUNE: Not him next door. Oh no. He wants money,
fifteen dollars. Why should I pay him? No sign's out
there, no license. If I go over to him, they might arrest
me!

SISSY: June. Do you want some bananas?

JUNE: I had a fungus toenail, you know. Sometimes
he grinds 'em down too short. Like it's fallin off or
something. My toes go on each other, too. He used to

put cotton on 'em. That won't help. He's, Oy, Jesus. He has my feet a mess.

SISSY: Ba-na-nas? Do you want?

JUNE: Yay-yuh! Oh, aren't you a big help!

(SISSY *takes the bananas.*)

JUNE: And an apple, Sissy!

(*An apple appears and is snatched by* SISSY. *Then a bag of potato chips rears its ugly temptation and* JUNE *succumbs, plucking it from the fringe.*)

JUNE: (*To the audience*) Some chips. Shh. Don't tell the doctor. Not Wayne. Not that one. My family doctor.

(SISSY *returns.*)

JUNE: Wayne asked if I remembered Lena who used to work in his office there in his front room. Lena. Long stringy hair. She was a bum. She looked funny. She didn't know what she was doing. Makin tickets out with the wrong date and everything. He used to go after her. She's the one who started him on those pills. Nothing happened to her. He went to jail for a year. Bob and Valerie were supposed to take care of his dog and cats, that's why the doctor's helpin 'em out now. They didn't even do nothin. Me and Tom saw you comin to his house, walkin the dog. How did you end up doin that?

SISSY: (*Writing selected words on a coupon*) They were gonna put him to sleep. I felt bad for Spike so I said I'd walk him.

JUNE: It was so old and sick. He woulda died if you didn't take care of him. Aye.

SISSY: (*Pointing*) Do you need corn?

JUNE: Me and Tom were coming home and saw the cop cars and the sheriff takin him out with handcuffs on him. Tommy said, "That's the doctor."

SISSY: O K. Fresh up your memory on that now. *(She walks away.)*

JUNE: It was in the paper about him. I still have it where it was something about forty thousand dollars. He was fillin in his own prescriptions at the Medicine Shoppe. Fallin alseep cuttin somebody's toes. Did you see it?

(SISSY returns.)

SISSY: The whole city saw it.

JUNE: Sissy, you shouldn't walk away so much. Your pocketbook's in the cart. Aye, Jesus, anybody could grab it. *(Taking SISSY's arm)* Let's see if they have that jello with fruit in it. I believe that's better for you than pudding. Oh, Sissy. I was bringin food in from Giant when the plainclothesmen told me everything about Wayne. Wayne might get a couple months, it's his second offense, he might get a year. He did. He got a year. I told Wayne, "Watch yourself. There's plainclothesmen around here again". I didn't wanna go out, they were watchin me, too.

SISSY: To see what you're feeding the birds?

JUNE: He broke his parole. Must still be on parole now yet. That's why they're watchin him.

SISSY: They should hire you. You know what he's doing twenty-four hours a day.

Scene 5

(The following month. WAYNE is waiting just outside his home with his arms crossed, chewing gum aggressively. JUNE peeks out, holding some post office slips.)

JUNE: Did you put these slips under my door from ups?

WAYNE: No. The postman did. You need to pick
something up.

JUNE: Is it for me or you? Sometimes you sleep and
don't answer your bell, and they leave me your
packages. *(Approaching him)* Where were you at two
o'clock today when I rang your bell? I wanted you to
come down, they were towing my car.

(WAYNE blows a big bubble. It pops.)

JUNE: Well, you're worse than the kids. Standin out
here blowin bubbles. My car is gone now. It was
Tommy's car. He owed four thousand dollars. I was
gonna sell it. I have a bill here for nine hundred dollars
for the car.

WAYNE: *(With a gesture)* Throw it away. We're finished
with the car.

JUNE: I shoulda looked in that car. I was afraid to open
the door, the horn would blow, everyone would look.
And there was some good stuff in that car yet. A big
umbrella. A sun visor. That spare tire. Tommy had
a lotta stuff in there we coulda used. They'll sell that
themselves now. The guy from Chase. Buncha crooks. I
didn't sign nothin. I'm sick of signin something, then I
get in trouble.

WAYNE: *(Holding up the slips and pointing to her)* You
have a certified letter to sign for. *(Gesturing a signature)*

JUNE: Aye my god, where?

WAYNE: *(Pointing to the address)* Thirteenth Street.

JUNE: All the way on Thirteenth Street? How am I
gonna get up there?

WAYNE: I'll take you right now.

JUNE: No.

WAYNE: No? *(With gestures)* You don't go today,
they'll send it back where it came from. *(Pause)* What's

wrong? Don't you wanna go for a ride? You've been inside all day.

JUNE: I'll take a cab.

WAYNE: How much did that cab driver charge you last time?

JUNE: I'm gonna call a cab, and you better not cancel it this time. They'll stop coming to 1144.

WAYNE: *(With gestures)* Don't waste your money on a cab. Twenty bucks that cab driver charged you. Twenty down, and twenty back.

JUNE: Aye. He wanted more than that. I says, "This is all I have. How much do you need?"

WAYNE: *(So* JUNE *can read his lips)* I don't need a penny. I'm free.

*(*JUNE *reluctantly walks to* WAYNE's *car.)*

WAYNE: Sit in front.

JUNE: No, they'll think I'm hanging up with you.

WAYNE: Would that be so bad, June? You're breakin my heart.

Scene 6

(A small panel of wood pops out of the stage right hardwood wall. WAYNE *and* JUNE *stand by it, as if before a bank teller window.)*

WAYNE: *(To* JUNE*)* Your I D expired a year ago. *(Politely to unseen teller)* She didn't know that. She opened the account at the branch on Penn Street with that I D. We need her whole amount of Social Security in cash. Seven hundred fifty. She pays her bills in cash.

JUNE: Why did she have to look at it? No one else looks at it.

WAYNE: Shhhh.

JUNE: Oh, it's a mess. Every time the third came on a Sunday we used to get our Social Security checks on Friday. I didn't get nothing.

WAYNE: Your Social Security checks don't come in the mail anymore. The money goes directly to the bank. To your account. That's what this letter said. *(Pointing to the letter)* "Your Social Security paper checks will end."

JUNE: *(Loud, with great authority, to the teller)* Why did they change this for old people for? Why didn't they leave things the way they were? They sent checks to your house. What was the problem with that? Now it's electronical? *(To WAYNE)* I have to go to the bank? Whoever thought of that? That President? They believe he's turning the country into a social country. *(Pause)* Bush never did nothing like that. Bush gave me two raises. Bush gave me a raise every year with that Social Security check. You can't be good no more. *(Gesturing with her thumb to WAYNE for the teller to see)* All the bums get the breaks, ain't?

WAYNE: *(With a driving gesture)* Wanna drive yourself home?

JUNE: I'm gonna hitchhike. The way you drive. Ohhh. You rush around too much.

WAYNE: *(With outstretched hand)* Gimme your check.

JUNE: *(She hands it to him)* They're always changing something.

WAYNE: *(Handing back her check)* You need to sign it on the back, too.

JUNE: *(Signing)* I don't know why I'm signing this. I was O K the way I was. Aye my god. Tell me I have to go through this every month now. *(Loud, to the teller)* Why did they change everything like this! I don't know why they're doing this. Why don't they leave these things alone!

WAYNE: Shhh. You think it's the teller's fault?

JUNE: *(Quieter to* WAYNE*)* They don't know me here. Let's go to the other one. Downtown.

WAYNE: They don't speak English downtown. We'll spend all day in that line.

JUNE: *(Unaware of what* WAYNE *said)* The one on Penn Street. They know me over there.

WAYNE: *(Pointing to her I D)* They know you over there, but they never told you your I D expired.

JUNE: All this time I'm using this card. Why don't they make this a lifetime? The way things are today. I shoulda kept workin. I worked forty years and I live in a dump. I don't even have a T V. I was hit by the car, down here, at 10th and Penn, I got four hundred dollars, and that's how I got my T V. Not from you. I turn it on, and nothin comes on.

WAYNE: It's obsolete. It has dials.

JUNE: *(Responding to his dismissive energy)* That's a eighty-three. It's a good set. The cable guy said that can be hooked up yet. It's thirty dollars to connect it.

WAYNE: You don't like watchin T V at my place?

JUNE: *(Unaware of what he said)* You got it hooked up for them upstairs. In that nice apartment. Has a dishwasher up there. Lotta closets. Nice. Big. Big. Nice. Not like my place. The windas are bad. Doors bad. Nothin included. We moved in two people, now I'm one person. You coulda lowered that rent a couple bucks for me now I'm only one person.

WAYNE: *(To the teller)* Twenties are fine. *(Quietly to the teller)* Can I have another envelope?

(WAYNE *separates the money into two envelopes without* JUNE *seeing. He keeps one, and gives the other to her.*)

WAYNE: Here.

JUNE: Boy, they operate quick! *(To the teller)* Thank you! *(To* WAYNE*)* How much is in here?

WAYNE: *(Writing)* You have to get a new ID for next month.

JUNE: Oh, when will this trouble end?

(JUNE *starts counting her money.* WAYNE *blows another big bubble.*)

JUNE: N'wait. It's only six. Six fifty. Aye, they made a mistake. Let's go back.

(The bubble pops. JUNE *starts to walk back to the teller.* WAYNE *stops her.*)

WAYNE: *(Shaking his head)* No mistake.

JUNE: Where's my hundred dollars?

WAYNE: *(Writing)* We had to leave a hundred in the account. Or else they'll close it down.

(Pause)

JUNE: Oh, I don't wanna deal with a bank. They take a lotta interest offa mine. I keep puttin money in, it gets less and less. I had it up to two hundred, I looked, it was down to fifty. My god they take too much interest offa me.

WAYNE: You gotta watch those banks. They can't be trusted.

Scene 7

(WAYNE *cradles two large paper shopping bags from Giant, with a smaller one dangling from his hand. He escorts* JUNE *home.*)

JUNE: Pee-u. Piles of cat dirt. Last week I opened my door. Boom. Boy, it just felt like a barrel of manure that the farmer's put out. I was eatin peanut butter crackers. You ain't hungry when you smell that.

(WAYNE *hands* JUNE *the smaller bag and takes the larger bags to his house.* SISSY *is sitting on* JUNE's *folding chair with a slim booklet on her lap.)*

JUNE: Sissy! Were you waitin long? Oh, we had a lot of trouble with the bank and stuff. Wayne ran me up.

WAYNE: *(From his home)* Hi, Sissy.

SISSY: Hi.

WAYNE: I was gonna call you.

SISSY: You need me to watch the dog?

WAYNE: No, I have a stiff neck.

SISSY: Oh.

WAYNE: You think you could help?

SISSY: I could work on your neck.

WAYNE: What other services do you provide?

SISSY: Shiatsu. Deep muscle massage. That's it.

WAYNE: Gotcha. Maybe I'll giveya a call. Gotta go. I have a date.

(WAYNE *walks to his house and begins assembling a tower of canned beans.)*

JUNE: I can't go with him no more. If I see him have that tin cup, I'm not getting in the car with him again. Mary Jane Schwambach, she watches him. Sometimes she parks over here and waves at me. She musta seen me get in the car with him and wondered where the heck we're going. I only sat in back, so she shouldn't be jealous. See how they take notice? He goes for my cheek to kiss me sometimes.

SISSY: *(To herself)* Oh. Insanity.

JUNE: See how people watch me? See me goin in his house. I tell 'em, "I went over to get my rent receipt. What else do you wanna know?" I'm single. I don't know who thinks I'm stayin with him.

SISSY: Besides you, no one.

JUNE: At the bank they thought he was my husband.

SISSY: Mm-hmm. And he brings you along for an eye candy.

JUNE: They said, "Is that your husband?" I said, heck no!

SISSY: *(To herself)* They thought he was your son.

JUNE: He's handsome and all, but dark handsome. Dead eyes.

SISSY: *(To herself)* You need a mirror in this place.

JUNE: Wayne can't stand that Schwambach. What did she do to him? I forget what he called her on that tablet. So many dirty names. Aye. I wouldn't wanna tangle with that Wayne. Jesus mighty, does he get mad. I believe if he woulda seen her, he woulda killed her. *(Pause)* Here we stopped at Giant on the way home, I didn't ask to go shopping.

SISSY: I asked Wayne if he could take you shopping for your refrigerator. *(Writing selected words)* I can't go every week. People get injured and they need to see me right away.

(SISSY hands JUNE the pad. JUNE takes it, ignoring what's been written, and starts to fan herself with it.)

JUNE: Wayne didn't get no money out. I got fifty bucks out. Me. I only got a couple things. He said, "Oh, this was free." I paid for it!

SISSY: You paid for his groceries?

JUNE: *(Fanning herself)* Yay-yuh! Go with him, he'll get a hundred dollars groceries, and you'll pay. He took the bags off the counter, went out the door, and left me inside. That was a rotten trick.

SISSY: Don't go shopping with him again. I'll take you.

JUNE: N'wait.

(SISSY puts the booklet in JUNE's lap.)

SISSY: Look. I brought this for you.

JUNE: What's this? *(Reading)* Food stamps? No, I don't get those.

SISSY: You qualify. *(Writing)* We have to fill out this application.

JUNE: I can pay for my food.

SISSY: *(Pointing to a question)* Are you a citizen of the United States?

JUNE: *(Glancing at the question)* I'm a senior citizen, but I don't vote.

(SISSY points to another question.)

JUNE: *(Reading)* Are-you-a-farm-worker? No. What the heck?

SISSY: Read this.

JUNE: *(Taking off her glasses)* Take mine off. I can read sometimes better. No. I don't get S S I. Just Social Security and pension.

SISSY: *(Pointing)* Write your name. *(Pointing)* Have you ever received food stamps from another state?

JUNE: No. Up their ass.

SISSY: *(Pointing)* How long did you attend school?

JUNE: Eighth grade. Aye my god, if we have to fill all this in. I wanna pay for my food.

SISSY: *(Pointing)* Do you have an Access card?

JUNE: Must I get my birth certificate out? Aye Jesus, if this ain't a mess.

SISSY: *(Pointing to a question)* Do you have a driver's license?

JUNE: How do Puerto Ricans get it? Do they go through all this? I'm gonna ask Peedro.

SISSY: That's a great question to ask Pedro if you never want to see him again. What county were you born in?

JUNE: United States.

SISSY: *(Underlining the word)* No, county?

JUNE: *(Unfamiliar with the word)* County?

SISSY: *(Pointing to a different question)* City of birth?

JUNE: Reading.

SISSY: *(Filling in a few blanks)* That's Berks County.

JUNE: *(To SISSY)* What city were you born in?

SISSY: *(Writing)* Patras. Greece.

JUNE: *(Confused)* Aye.

SISSY: *(Elaborating as she fills in a few more blanks)* If I were a man I would've stayed. Men are kings. They call it: almataki. Little Statue. That Chinese man invented a little statue. It doesn't bend. It doesn't stop. It's a vacuum cleaner. No foreplay. No skin against you. You have an orgasm in thirty seconds. *(Pointing)* Mother's full maiden name?

JUNE: Anna Fausnacht.

SISSY: *(Turning to a new page)* Now, this page.

JUNE: Throw that booklet out!

SISSY: No. We're gonna finish this. We're almost done. *(Pointing to the next question)* Have you ever had a drug problem?

JUNE: Drug problem? *(Pointing)* Over here, next door.
Not me. Noooooo.

SISSY: *(Handing June the application)* Read this.

JUNE: Gimme that pen. *(Reading)* Disabled this and that.
Skip some of that. That's a crime right there. I can't
stand it. That's enough to drive me to drink.

SISSY: *(Pointing)* Do you drive a truck or a motorcycle?

JUNE: *(Glancing at the question)* Oh, I never heard of this.
A truck or a motorcycle? And they wanna know if I'm
on drugs yet? Tell 'em I'm innocent. I'm the only one
who doesn't drink in the building. That's it.

SISSY: *(Pointing)* Place of employment?

JUNE: Quinlan's Pretzel Bakery. Forty years if you need
that yet.

SISSY: *(Pointing)* What did you do there?

JUNE: Machine operator. Put dough in the hoppers. The
machine changed shapes, made all different pretzels.
You put different nozzles on. Long penny rods. Kids
used to come on tours. Get free samples. Tiny twins.
Pretzel sticks. Everyday, different machinery, put
different heads on. Had to get on time. I got on fast.
They didn't have anyone with me long. Took the
helper right away. I didn't need help.

SISSY: How much pension?

JUNE: You had to order the dough. If you had bad
dough it would come out wrong. The baker downstairs
told me, "I could tell when you were on the machines".
When I wasn't on, there were no pretzels on the belt!

SISSY: *(Pointing)* Fill this in—

JUNE: Tom worked at Quinlan's, that's where I met
him. Yay-yuh. He used to load the trailers. Big tractor
trailers. That was a hard job, too, sometimes. He was a
good worker. He used to work Saturdays and Sundays,

straight through seven days a week. He worked thirty,
thirty-five years. *(Totally lost in thought)* Rosie said,
"Over there's that guy. He's watchin you. He don't
belong over here. He belongs in the shipping room."
That was Tom. My Tommy. *(Pause)* Just put machine
operator.

(SISSY *closes the application.*)

Scene 8

(SISSY *walks over to meet* WAYNE *who is already in her
home.*)

SISSY: Hi, Wayne. Before we start I have to ask you a
few questions.

WAYNE: O K.

SISSY: Are you on any medications?

WAYNE: Why?

SISSY: If you're on steroids, steroids take calcium from
the bones, so I cannot put much pressure on the back
and the rib cage.

(Pause)

WAYNE: I'm not on steroids.

SISSY: Are you exercising?

WAYNE: You're starting to sound like my girlfriend
now. She doesn't understand, I preserve my energy for
important things.

SISSY: June asks you about the gym?

(SISSY *turns her back, and walks to her massage mat on the
floor.* WAYNE *follows.*)

SISSY: Let's get started. Lie on your stomach, please.

WAYNE: Should I take off my shoes?

SISSY: Yes.

(WAYNE *takes off his shoes.)*

WAYNE: Should I take off my pants?

SISSY: No.

WAYNE: They're a little tight. I'd be more comfortable.

SISSY: *(Indifferent)* Go right ahead.

(WAYNE *takes his pants off. His choice of underwear is
surprising: it has a print of lolling tongues. He lies down on
his stomach.)*

WAYNE: You want me to put my face in this hole?

SISSY: Yes. Make yourself comfortable.

WAYNE: I'm comfortable with that, you know?

SISSY: With what?

WAYNE: *(Snickering)* Nothing. *(He lies down on his
stomach. His face disappears in the donut cushion.)*

SISSY: Bend your arms. Put them above your shoulders.

(WAYNE *puts his arms in an odd position.)*

WAYNE: Where do you want my arms?

(SISSY *repositions* WAYNE's *arms and starts working on his
back, gently massaging in circular motions to loosen up the
muscles.)*

WAYNE: *(Raising his head)* What about the front?

SISSY: We'll get to the front.

(WAYNE *drops his face back into the cushion.* SISSY *now
applies firm thumb pressure down the meridians of his spine.
He starts to moan.)*

SISSY: Is that too much pressure?

WAYNE: No, you have god's hands. Don't stop.

SISSY: Put your arms on your sides.

(WAYNE *does, awkwardly.*)

SISSY: With the palms up. Relax the muscles.

(SISSY *gently shakes out* WAYNE'*s arms, and shifts up to his neck, working the meridians from the base of the neck out to the shoulders.*)

SISSY: Your neck is very tight.

WAYNE: I know. I need a release.

SISSY: What kind of pillow do you use?

WAYNE: For what?

SISSY: To sleep.

WAYNE: I don't know. Regular.

SISSY: A pillow with feathers doesn't accomplish anything because it turns into nothing from the weight of your head.

WAYNE: I have a silk pillowcase.

SISSY: Good.

(SISSY *moves from the shoulder down the arm, pressing meridians along the way to the elbow.* WAYNE *lifts his arm off the mat and squeezes her hand. She pulls away.*)

SISSY: Turn on your back, please.

(WAYNE *turns on his back.*)

SISSY: There's a stretch you can do in the morning to help your neck. Take your hand, and tilt it toward the shoulder. With the nose facing the ceiling.

WAYNE: Show me.

(SISSY *picks up* WAYNE'*s right hand and slaps it onto his right ear, pushing his head left with a lot of sudden force. He responds by sitting up and trying to kiss her. She stands up.*)

SISSY: We're finished here.

WAYNE: O K. You're the boss. But I'm not paying you for this.

SISSY: No kidding.

WAYNE: *(Putting on his pants)* Whatever this witch doctor crap is. I've been misled.

SISSY: Goodbye, Wayne.

Scene 9

(A month later. JUNE is walking around her apartment cleaning. At the entrance, just inside, WAYNE is eerily watching her. She finally notices him.)

JUNE: Oh. What are you doing back there?

(WAYNE doesn't move.)

JUNE: Well, c'mon in. *(Fluffing her hair)* There're no men in here.

(WAYNE still does not move. JUNE approaches him, assuming he's preoccupied with the junk from the upstairs tenants in the vestibule.)

JUNE: Don't they make you sick with all this stuff? What do they have out? Oh, a bunch a junk. Makes the whole place look so sloppy. I used to have that hallway nice and clean. I used to wash the woodwork and everything. Looks like the city dump now, aye. I wanted to ask you about the hospital chair.

(WAYNE starts walking away from JUNE into her living room.)

JUNE: I think the hospital wants it back. I can't throw it out. I'll get in trouble.

(JUNE follows WAYNE.)

WAYNE: That chair is a toilet. Nobody wants it back.

JUNE: He only used it a couple times.

WAYNE: *(With a gesture)* Throw it out.

JUNE: What if the hospital sends me a bill for it? I'm in enough trouble. That car was in my name, I still get bills. Aye-yayeyaye. *(She laughs.)* I'm half dead-sick. I don't know why I'm laughing. I was eatin one a those ice cream sandwiches and I got it on my top. *(Straightening things out as she walks)* I just emptied my wastebasket and sprayed it.

(WAYNE picks up the lid of a cookie jar and peers inside. Nothing)

JUNE: Where's Spike?

WAYNE: *(Visibly upset)* He's gone.

JUNE: Oh, Wayne. He passed? Well, it's better for him now. He was in a lot of pain.

(WAYNE writes on JUNE's pad.)

WAYNE: *(Showing her the pad)* Don't you need to go to the bank to pick up your Social Security?

JUNE: *(Glancing at the pad)* Sissy took me already.

(WAYNE is shocked.)

JUNE: What's wrong?

WAYNE: *(Writing)* You don't wanna go with me anymore?

JUNE: *(Glancing at the pad)* I already went.

(WAYNE writes, and hands the pad back to JUNE.)

JUNE: *(Reading)* "Any-new-tall-tales-about-me? Liars-aren't-smart-enough-to-ask-if-true." *(Looking at WAYNE)* What are you pickin on me for?

WAYNE: I'm not picking on you. I'm telling you, they don't want you to go with me.

JUNE: Me? Who?

WAYNE: *(Pointing)* You. You. They don't want you to
go with me. *(Writing)* People are telling lies about me.
They're making it bad for me. You only go shopping
with Sissy. They told you to stay away from me. They
want you turned against me.

JUNE: Who?

WAYNE: Schwambach.

JUNE: I don't bother with her.

WAYNE: *(Writing)* I want none of my affairs to be
discussed or even hinted at with Schwambach. I had to
pay an extreme price for trusting in her.

JUNE: *(Glancing at the pad)* I don't know her. I have
nothin to do with that.

(WAYNE continues writing.)

JUNE: Don't get me in with that. What brought this up?
Did she say somethin that's stickin in you?

WAYNE: *(Showing JUNE the pad)* Why doesn't she tell the
truth about me once? I feel like going down there after
her.

JUNE: *(Glancing at the pad)* Ooh, you're on a war path
now. Now you're gettin me nervous and worked up.
Go to sleep or something.

WAYNE: *(Writing)* What did Sissy tell you?

JUNE: *(Glancing at the pad)* You're gonna drag Sissy in,
too? What started all this? Nobody's talkin about you.
I don't listen to nobody. *(Pause)* You have too much
time on your hands, Wayne. You need a job. *(She gets
an unframed, folded certificate.)* You see this? *(Unfolding
it)* "Bakery, Confec-shi-airy, and Tobacco Workers
International Union: 25 Year Membership Award."
(Pause) You don't get this for nothing. You have to be
a good worker and a steady worker. I was gonna get
a frame for that, but I don't get much. *(Pause)* Well, if

I wasn't good, you think they woulda kept me forty
years? That was my first job and my last one. See this
watch? *(She takes it off her wrist, showing the engraving on
the back)* "39 years." It's supposed to say "40". I had to
watch that shop steward. He engraved "39". He was
drinkin and stuff. I was there forty years. He said, "Oh,
I'm sorry." "Well, you messed me up." I know how
long I worked there. Boy, that was a mix-up. *(Folding
the certificate)* Why don't you get a mechanic job like
Peedro? You're always on a vacation. You ain't workin
since you used to trim toenails.

WAYNE: You make it sound like I worked in a fucking
nail salon. *(Writing)* I would still be a doctor if it wasn't
for Schwambach.

JUNE: Her again?

(WAYNE writes for an extended period of time.)

JUNE: Oh, you're writing a whole letter now. Are you
crying?

*(WAYNE stops writing, and crumbles up the piece of paper.
He stares at JUNE for a second and writes a new note.)*

JUNE: *(Reading)* "Do-you-have-$100?" Already? This
is only the beginning of the month. Look at you. You
owe me twenty dollars. Tom's car had a flat tire. You
said, "Give me $20, I'll fix it." You took the money,
and never fixed it. Now it's too late, the car's gone,
you never put that tire on, and I'm outta twenty bucks.
Ain't that a big deal?

WAYNE: *(Writing)* Don't you have $70?

JUNE: *(Glancing at the pad)* You must think I'm Miss
America or something. I don't have seventy dollars.
I'm payin my bills, I got nothin leftover for you.

WAYNE: *(Writing)* How bout 50?

JUNE: *(Glancing at the pad)* Oh, you'll have me bankrupt yet. I only get paid once a month.

WAYNE: *(Writing)* Don't you have any extra money that you don't need right now?

JUNE: *(Glancing at the pad)* Any extra money? That I don't need? Heck no! You can get your father's money. You ain't gettin mine.

WAYNE: I'm good for it. I can give you this card.

(A white credit card appears miraculously suspended in the black fringe.)

JUNE: No, get that card away from me.

WAYNE: Here, just take this card.

JUNE: Stop following me around with that card, you hear? I don't want that card. I don't use credit cards.

WAYNE: You can get your money back with this card.

(WAYNE moves toward JUNE.)

JUNE: No, you're not comin in here. That ain't allowed.

(WAYNE stops. He remains a step lower than JUNE.)

JUNE: You're gettin fresh now. You think you're gonna walk into my bedroom yet?

WAYNE: Let me borrow money. You'll get all of it back and more with this card.

JUNE: No, I don't have a credit card and I don't want one. You better be careful. You ended up in jail using other people's credit cards. I'm not gonna end up in jail with you.

WAYNE: Schwambach made that up about her card! This card has nothing to do with her! This is just so you can get your money!

JUNE: You want money. You're askin me for money. Why don't you keep that card and get money yourself?

Why don't you stick it up your rear end while your at it.

(JUNE *plucks the card off the fringe and throws it at* WAYNE. *He slithers on the ground and puts the card in his mouth, as he takes her clock radio from her tray table, cradling it home in his arms.*)

Scene 10

(*A month later. A single birthday card is now propped up where* JUNE's *clock radio used to be. She plucks a panel of carpet out of her wall, and reveals an air conditioner. She turns it on while* SISSY *stands in her home with a small paper gift bag extended.*)

SISSY: Happy Birthday!

JUNE: Oh! You didn't have to do that. I knew you were up to no good. Do you want some mashed potatoes and gravy? It's all in a can, I just have to heat it up.

SISSY: No, thank you.

JUNE: You don't eat enough. You should sit down and eat.

SISSY: *(Writing)* Your hair looks nice.

JUNE: Yeah, I look good. I didn't get outta the hairdresser till 11:30. *(Fussing with her hair)* Debbie had 'em up a little too high, I didn't like that.

(SISSY *notices a card on* JUNE's *table. She picks it up.*)

JUNE: Cathy sent me that card. When I looked, and got that card, I was so surprised. She might come up with the boys for a couple days.

SISSY: Let's hold our breath for Cathy who never comes.

(JUNE *walks toward her newly installed air conditioner. Her hair billows from upward jets of air.*)

JUNE: I'm afraid to keep runnin that. It says eighty. That's too high. Put it down to sixty. It'll go up to two hundred dollars yet.

SISSY: Eighty is cheaper for air conditioning.

JUNE: I can take heat better than cold. I worked in front of ovens all those years in the heat. What's gonna happen to my electric bill? Wayne's gonna pay that, not me.

(WAYNE *turns off the air conditioner.*)

SISSY: Good luck. *(Writing)* Did you show him my note?

JUNE: *(Glancing at the pad)* Aye. Wayne read those notes, ripped 'em up and put 'em in the wastebasket. That's how he went. *(Sticking her tongue out)* Stuck his tongue out. Threw 'em out.

SISSY: He grew up in a cave by wolves. Very quiet. Very low key wolves.

JUNE: I said, "Read those two notes Sissy left here for you." He said, "Does she really need it?" See, what Schwambach did to him, he can't get work.

SISSY: I'll never see that money. At least you won't be fainting anymore. People die from the heat.

JUNE: I'm too disgusted with this place. He comes in when I'm not home. Since Tom ain't here. He knows I'm alone now. I'm gettin tired of it. I come in, I always gotta look to see. I know what I have here. Oh, I went in there for that little radio. That was gone. I wonder what next he's gonna take. He's always stickin stuff in his pockets. Snoopin around my drawers and all. He watches where I get my money from, too, when I have it under here— *(Raising a doily)* I gotta watch, and put it in the closet. In my safety box. I never count money when he's around. He's gettin pretty shrewd. Look at these rotten pens. He stole the good pens. *(Looking for a pen in her purse)* Tom, every time he paid his insurance he got this pen. *(Her hand emerges with a pen; she clicks it a few times)* Nice pen. Wayne took three of these. Here, I don't get this out when he's here. My good pen. *(Putting it back in her purse)* He can use this junk he brought over. Half of 'em don't write. This is what he brought over. *(Holding up a handful of ancient pens and pencil stubs)* Look at this junk. *(Lifting her placemats to show things she's hiding)* Look he didn't see this. My napkin holder. I put that together myself. Look at the stuff he's doin. All my things are disappearing. He doesn't know I have money back in that closet. Toilet tissue, my little Christmas Jeṣus clock. If he saw I had all that, he'd come in and carry it all out. I can tell when he had the dog in, the rugs are messed up and all. Pokey. Did you see his new dog?

SISSY: *(Nodding)* Pookey, not Pokey.

JUNE: Yeah, big. Black fur. Black eyes. He brought him over here on a new lease and all. Waving his tail. I gave him ham, you shoulda seen how nice he took it.

(SISSY takes a Chinese linament out of her purse and rubs her temples with it.)

JUNE: Oh, that smells strong. Is that medicine?

(SISSY hands JUNE the bottle. JUNE looks at it.)

JUNE: That's Chinese, ain't?

SISSY: Everybody has headaches. I don't. I rub myself with linaments. I cannot sleep with anyone. That's what has saved me. I'm alone.

JUNE: *(Putting the bottle closer to her nose)* Ooh, that burns your nose up! Don't let Wayne get a hold a that! *(Tilting back the bottle and imitating drinking sounds)* "Blp, blp, blp." He'd guzzle it down.

(JUNE *hands the bottle back to* SISSY *and heads to her bathroom.*)

JUNE: My sink's always breaking. I have to wash my dishes in the bathroom sink. I'll be right out. *(From her bathroom)* Peedro helped me. He stopped it running the other day. He said, I'm payin too much for one person. Nothin included, but the trash. All this goes wrong. *(Re-entering)* Peedro showed me some apartments on Franklin Street cheaper than this. I might move there. They don't charge you no money down.

SISSY: *(Writing)* You have to tell Wayne about your sink.

JUNE: *(Glancing at the note)* He knows. We just had a plumber in last month. He don't pay 'em. No plumber wants to come here.

SISSY: *(Pointing at* JUNE'*s kitchen)* What's that?

(JUNE *looks towards her kitchen.*)

JUNE: Aye! What are they doin upstairs? It's a leak from upstairs.

SISSY: *(Pointing)* It's not from upstairs. Look. It's your sink.

JUNE: Call Wayne.

(SISSY *picks up the phone and dials.*)

JUNE: He was just under the sink yesterday. Now a damn pipe or something broke.

SISSY: *(Into phone)* Wayne, there's an emergency with June's kitchen.

(JUNE *takes the phone from* SISSY.)

JUNE: *(Into phone)* Wayne, get over here, the kitchen's fillin up with hot water. Steamin and steamin. You better get over here and call the plumber. You didn't gimme my rent receipt either. I better get my rent receipt, I'm paid up for the month. I told Debbie.

(JUNE *hands the phone back to* SISSY.)

JUNE: What's he saying?

SISSY: He hung up.

(WAYNE *enters with a roll of paper towels. June recognizes them immediately.*)

JUNE: Those are my paper towels! You took those off my kitchen counter. I yelled at you and you just kept walkin'.

WAYNE: I needed paper towels. (*From the living room, he rips a single paper towel off the roll, and frisbees it onto the kitchen floor.*)

JUNE: That all you're gonna do?

WAYNE: (*To* SISSY) She doesn't know how to use the garbage disposal.

JUNE: You need to go downstairs.

WAYNE: No.

JUNE: Yes, you do, to shut the electric off. That's where the boxes are.

SISSY: You better call the plumber.

WAYNE: (*Throwing more paper towels*) I can take care of it.

SISSY: This is a serious problem. You need a professional.

WAYNE: What's the plumber gonna tell me that I don't already know? (*Writing on* JUNE's *pad*) Stop using the garbage disposal. (*He walks back to his home and sits down.*)

JUNE: *(Glancing at the pad)* I didn't use that garbage disposal since the plumber was here. *(She exits to her kitchen.)*

SISSY: Wayne, it's her birthday today. This is what she does for her birthday. Sits and looks at the walls. That's it. The least you could do is make sure her place is livable.

WAYNE: It's hard for me right now. Since I lost my practice, I'm in a hole.

SISSY: Well, if you don't start taking care of her place, she'll move out, and no one else is gonna move in there.

WAYNE: She always says that.

SISSY: She was looking at another apartment. On Franklin Street. She's serious about finding another place.

(JUNE returns. WAYNE writes on a paper towel.)

WAYNE: Where are you moving?

JUNE: *(Looking at SISSY)* Aye.

WAYNE: *(Writing)* Are you moving in with your boyfriend, Pedro?

JUNE: *(To SISSY)* You told him!

SISSY: No, June. *(She writes on the pad.)*

JUNE: OH!

SISSY: June.

JUNE: You're two-faced! You're TALKIN ABOUT ME!

SISSY: *(Handing June the pad)* I was trying to help you.

JUNE: *(Stepping back from SISSY)* Why would you talk about me like that? I'm not tellin nothin in back of your back. I'm tellin your face. YOU'RE A

TROUBLEMAKER! I DON'T WANT NOTHIN TO DO
WITH YOU!

SISSY: O K. *(Dropping* JUNE's *keys on the table)* Here are
your keys. *(To* WAYNE*)* I guess I'm fired.

Scene 11

(A month later. WAYNE *is sitting at his table with green
rubber dish-washing gloves on, sorting coins. His table is
covered with stacks of overflowing loose pennies, bottles of
A-Treat orange soda, Swiss Cake Rolls, a clear plastic bag of
blue cotton candy. Yellowed obituary clippings with paw-
print borders overwhelm a bulletin board. A plaque reads:
"Cats are like potato chips. You can't have just one."* JUNE
approaches him.)

JUNE: Where were you?

WAYNE: *(With a dismissive gesture)* I was here.

You should come over. It smells terrible. You shouldn't
let them keep so many cats upstairs.

WAYNE: I'm not coming over there to smell it all the
time. *(With a gesture)* I'll call 'em.

JUNE: The smell draws into to my apartment, I ain't
puttin up with that. I was sick. And you keep your
door locked. You don't want nobody walkin in, you
said, but you walk in and out of my place any old
time. *(Pause)* Why do you have gloves on? *(She walks
forward.)* That's a dumb place for that water dish. You
step right in it yet.

WAYNE: I never did.

JUNE: *(Bending over to wipe off her shoe)* Oh, you put junk
down there for the cats, too. What is that? Tuna? Boy,
I was standing there ringin and ringin your bell. Aye
my god. Why don't you answer your door? Are you in
trouble again?

WAYNE: I'm not in trouble. *(Writing on a paper towel)*
They just wanted to leave me a note.

JUNE: *(Glancing at the note)* A sheriff and two police
cars?

WAYNE: *(Writing)* Do you have two nickels for a dime?

JUNE: *(Glancing at the note)* No. I don't have no quarters
neither.

(WAYNE writes a second note.)

JUNE: *(Reading)* "Do-you-have-batt-ries? I-need-batt-
ries-for-my-clock-radio." Your radio! That's mine! You
stole it.

WAYNE: I didn't steal anything. It was laying there.

JUNE: Tom used to sit in that front room and play that.
It plays good, my little radio. I didn't see it till I went
for it. Then it disappeared.

WAYNE: *(Writing)* You can't hear anyway, what do you
want with it?

JUNE: *(Glancing at the note)* Tom gave me that clock
for my birthday! You're the only one in there. You
shouldn't be carryin my stuff out.

(WAYNE gets JUNE's clock radio, and gives it to her.)

WAYNE: *(Visibly upset)* I'm sorry.

JUNE: Oh, don't be a sourpuss now. You took my radio
and you returned it. That's not a big deal. You want to
make it up to me, go down to 9th and Penn and pick
up my pills.

WAYNE: *(Intrigued; writing)* What kind of pills?

JUNE: *(Glancing at the note)* My water pills and
cholesterol.

WAYNE: *(Disappointed)* Oh.

JUNE: I can't go down and get 'em. I thought my head was comin off. I was tryin to clean out the microwave, but I do a little bit, then sit back down, then get up, and do it again. Somethin ain't right. I'm sick, I can't get out. Here I was sitting on my chair. I couldn't get up. I even thought I was gonna throw up, and I didn't throw up. I had such pain. In the stomach, or it's the new pills Dr Manyabay give me, I don't know. I had diarrhea last week, broke out in a sweat, then I got the chills. Wasn't like that before. Yay-yuh, uh-huh. I don't know if it's down in my ovaries or what. I had soup. And then, like gas pains. That's what they are. Threw up my eggs. I had the raisin bread. I don't know about raisin stuff. I'm afraid to tell my doctor since I had that tumor.

WAYNE: *(Writing)* Didn't you tell your doctor you've been having trouble sleeping?

JUNE: *(Glancing at the note)* That was only from the heat that I had trouble.

WAYNE: *(Writing)* The doctor can give you something to help.

JUNE: *(Glancing at the note)* I don't need help. With the air condition I sleep right through. If I was sick, I was gonna call 9-eleven. Nobody was around here. I was waitin for Peedro to come around. He took my dresser away yesterday.

WAYNE: *(With a money gesture)* Did you pay him?

JUNE: No, I give it to him. Geez. He left right away. He don't hang around or nothin. He put that table together for me. He said it was a good table. Strong wood. He lifted that up just like it was a feather, turned it upside down. I couldn't ask you to do that. You're pretty unhandy around the house yet.

WAYNE: Talk to Pedro outside. Don't bring him in your house all the time. *(Writing)* He's looking to take advantage of you.

JUNE: *(Glancing at the note)* Peedro's not fresh. He never made a pass at me.

WAYNE: *(Annoyed at the misunderstanding)* Not like that!

JUNE: You think I'm hangin up with him? You watch everything in and out, standing on the porch and stuff. Next time I know you're lookin, I'll go over and sit on his lap.

WAYNE: *(Writing)* He wants something from you.

JUNE: *(Glancing at the note)* He doesn't do nothin. I don't care what you say. *(She laughs.)* Even when I'm sick, I laugh. I'm no sourpuss. When I feel, I just laugh and be happy. I'm broke, I laugh. What good is money if you can't buy nothin?

(WAYNE offers a new note on the paper towel.)

JUNE: *(Ignoring the paper towel)* Oh. I had the chills and all so bad. I never got that way. Never. Ohh. Aye, oooh. Not since that operation hurt me down in there yet. They took that tumor outta me. I was in bad shape. I went in there it was bloody, my urine. I don't get my period.

WAYNE: *(Holding up the paper towel)* June! Enough!

JUNE: *(Misunderstanding his energy)* Aye my god, it gushed outta me. Here it was a tumor. It burst in my bladder. I was terrible sick. They had me in a wheelchair and took me down. They put that thing on my face, I didn't know nothing, then I woke up. The doctors said, "You went through it good." The surgery, when I woke up. Tom brought me home. I couldn't put my legs up. It hurt my insides. Doctor said, "Don't go up and down steps." I don't have steps. Just one to the bedroom. They sent me a bill for twenty-one thousand

dollars. Where are they gonna get that money? They
can open me up again, find it in my ovaries.

(WAYNE *flips his table over and exits.*)

JUNE: Oh. (*She finally reads the paper towel.*) "I-don't-
know-if-they'll-give-me-your-pills." Oh, don't worry,
Wayne. They won't give you no trouble. Say it's for
June Willitz and I'm sick. Don't tell 'em your name.
They mighta seen it in the papers.

Scene 12

(JUNE *parts the fringe to reveal* SISSY *in a bright summer
tank top.* SISSY *struts forward.*)

JUNE: (*About* SISSY's *top*) Oh, look at you! They'll see
you comin. (*Slight nervous cough*) I'm chewin cough
drops, gettin worse myself. Allergies. Look what
Wayne give me. (*She holds up a slip of paper.*) That's
a rent receipt: "Paid in full." I thought he didn't
appreciate nothin, then he goes and does that. Wayne
said I didn't have to pay my rent for the month because
of what he owes me. I'm paid up in rent for the month,
and I didn't have to pay it. Now I can give you that
money for the air condition myself. (*Holding up her
crooked index finger*) N'wait.

SISSY: Put down your ET finger. You're not paying me.

JUNE: I already give you forty. What do I owe you?

SISSY: He owes me, not you. June! I don't want your
money.

JUNE: (*Finding a wad of bills*) …Two forty-three. That
was my clock number at work. I'll never forget that.
(*She extends the wad of cash.*) He's a good man, after all,
ain't? I went over, he trimmed my toenails for free. He
walked down to 9th and Penn in the heat and picked
up my pills. He helped me with Tom. Checkin what

the nurses and stuff did when he was in the hospital
bed. He understood the pills and stuff which I didn't.
Got socks for him. Underwear. He liked Tom. He used
to come and talk when he was in bed. Oh, he cried
terrible when Tom died. That I must give him. *(Pause)*
Here, take this. Go on. You'll never see it from him.
Take it. You helped me too much. You got me that
food stamp card. You can use that, too, you know. To
get that milk you get with almonds, your kinda milk.
I have a coupon for that. Get one, get three free. Yeah,
that's not just for me. I wouldn't have that card if it
wasn't for you. You can get whatever you want with
that.

SISSY: *(Shaking her head)* Stop it. I'm not using your food
stamps.

JUNE: I'm sorry, Sissy. You did so much for me. You're
like family to me. Take this, or I won't feel right.

(SISSY takes the money.)

SISSY: Thank you, June. I appreciate that.

JUNE: What are you doing now? Are you working?

SISSY: *(With gesture)* I have two more people.

JUNE: Do you wanna come down? I'm just sitting there
by myself. I was stayin in, in case Cathy come down
with the boys.

SISSY: *(Pointing to her watch)* I can't. My next client is
coming.

JUNE: You don't have to run around. You have enough
to do. N'wait. *(Digging into her purse)* I have to show
you this letter. He goes through my mail. He said I
missed an important letter from the insurance. My
policy lapsed and he helped me write out the check to
send it. I didn't know what the policy was. It was an A
D policy. All I have is A A R P. *(Handing SISSY the letter)*
What's this policy? I don't know what it is.

SISSY: *(To herself)* Let me see. A D? What's A ? *(Reading forms)* Accidental Death. Change of Beneficiary.

JUNE: Wayne said after Tom died we had to update that insurance. He filled out the forms for me and all yet.

SISSY: *(To herself)* Oh my God. June. *(To JUNE)* Do you know what this is?

JUNE: *(Glancing at the pad)* He put his name down, so they can call him, like they did with the car.

SISSY: Wayne named himself as a beneficiary. *(Writing)* If you die in an accident, he'll get a hundred and fifty thousand dollars. Why did you sign this?

JUNE: *(Pausing to read)* I didn't know that's what it was.

SISSY: *(Writing)* You have to cancel this immediately.

JUNE: Aye, it's gettin worse around here. How do I cancel it?

SISSY: *(Taking out her cell phone)* You can never sign anything from Wayne.

JUNE: What is he up to? That nitwit.

SISSY: *(Into phone)* Yes, I'm calling about the A D policy of June Willitz. Policy number: 67309.

JUNE: I knew he was a crook! I can't get no paper on the corner no more. Oh, when I went up to the corner and seen that sign: "Stop Stealing," I just about fell over. The box is empty now. Yeah, the crook.

SISSY: *(Into phone)* She's deaf. She needs to cancel her policy. She has no beneficiaries. Her husband is dead. Wayne Hinnershitz is not her husband. He's her landlord. What does she have to do?

JUNE: Oh Sissy, everything happens to us. The good ones. The bums. Nothin happens to them.

SISSY: *(Into phone)* What does the letter need to say? *(Jotting down)* Mm-hmm. O K. Thank you. *(She hangs up; to* JUNE*)* We have a letter to write.

Scene 13

*(*WAYNE *pushes a large, realistic wall into place at the downstage edge of his linoleum floor, complete with a front door that can swing open on hinges. He exits.* SISSY *walks in front of this new outer facade on her way to* JUNE*'s home.)*

SISSY: *(Writing)* You sent that letter?

JUNE: Yeah, it went off to 13th Street yesterday.

SISSY: *(Writing)* Did you tell Wayne you cancelled it?

JUNE: Yay-yuh. I told him when I give him the letter. I said, "Sissy told me I don't need that insurance, and this cancels it."

SISSY: *(Incredulous; writing)* You gave him the letter?

JUNE: He run it up to the post office himself. He mails cards to Cathy all the time. Maybe he didn't mail the last one. If he did, I would've gotten an answer by now. I should've asked if the boys got promoted to the 4th grade.

SISSY: *(Writing)* Are you sure Wayne sent the letter?

JUNE: Aye, I saw him drive away. I'll ask him when he gets home.

SISSY: *(With a gesture)* Don't ask him for Christsake.

JUNE: He shoulda come home today. Sometimes he leaves Pokey six or eight hours alone. That dog misses Wayne.

SISSY: We have to call the insurance in a few days to make sure they got it.

JUNE: Where's the doctor anyway?

(SISSY *shrugs.*)

JUNE: He's probably doin drugs with his thermos on Carsonia. He's not with his family this long. He can't stand his mother more than a day.

(SISSY *gets up.*)

SISSY: Goodnight, June.

JUNE: It's all dark over there. Pokey's been alone all day in the dark. I don't know why he got a new dog. He's never home with it. Did he ask you to walk it?

SISSY: *(Shaking her head)* No.

JUNE: How's the dog there for two days with nobody walkin it?

(SISSY *shrugs.*)

JUNE: Do you still have a key to his place?

(SISSY *barely nods.*)

JUNE: We should check on Pokey. Make sure he has enough food. Maybe he needs to go for a walk. Sissy, the poor dog. Oh.

SISSY: *(Reluctantly)* O K.

JUNE: Let me find my shoes. I can't wear these slippers outside they have holes in 'em. *(Putting on her shoes)* I'll vacc-yim tomorrow.

(JUNE *and* SISSY *walk to* WAYNE's *front door.* SISSY *puts the key in the door and opens it. They step in and close the door behind them.*)

JUNE: *(From behind the wall)* Pokey. Where are you, Pokey? Pokey.

SISSY: *(From behind the wall)* Pookey is his name. *(Suddenly the jingling of a chain collar and dogs tags can be heard from a distance. The sounds get closer and burst into vicious barking.)*

JUNE: Pokey, mind! No, Pokey. No, no, no!

(SISSY *pops out, gasping, and pulls the door closed behind her.* JUNE *remains behind the wall.*)

SISSY: June! *(She tries the door handle. It locked automatically when the door closed.)* June! *(She fumbles for her keys.)* June? Are you O K?

(JUNE *emerges from the other side, dressed in finer clothes than she ever wore when she was alive.*)

JUNE: I'm fine. Don't worry about me. I'm leavin' this dump. It's too many hangs around here. I'm goin' to see my sister. Tom packed a lunch for us. We're drivin' out to visit her. She feels better, I can tell. She has a nice home, trailer and all. Two bathrooms. A nice trailer, looks like a house. Wouldn't believe it was a trailer. Looks like a beautiful house. Stairs and stuff.

SISSY: Oh no.

JUNE: It was good you pulled that door shut, Sissy. That woulda been the end of you. I didn't think he'd go for me. He knew me. He didn't know you. Yeah, he stood up. He was ready to jump on you. Rooooh! And he's big. If he jumped on you, he'd knock you over. They said he was layin alone at Animal Rescue, maybe that's why they put him alone. I heard him barking the other day, somebody went to pet him, Wayne says, "He won't bite ya." I was gonna say, "Oh, yes he will." He is an, aye. He's enough to kill somebody. *(She starts to walk away.)* Tommy, those sirloin patties make a good sandwich. So tender. *(She exits.)*

Scene 14

(WAYNE *enters and confronts* SISSY *by his front door.*)

SISSY: Wayne, I don't know what to tell you. June wanted to check on Pookey. I never thought this would happen. *(Breaking into tears)* I panicked. I just.

WAYNE: *(Suspicious)* What did you do?

SISSY: *(In tears)* What?

WAYNE: What really happened?

SISSY: *(In tears)* Nothing. It was an accident.

WAYNE: Then why are you crying?

(SISSY *cries, unable to speak.*)

WAYNE: I understand. Look, sometimes it's hard to admit things. Let me make it easier for you. You got fed up doing your charity work, it's O K. You're only human.

SISSY: *(In tears)* No. I loved June.

WAYNE: I only wish you didn't involve Pookey. They're talking about putting him down now. My boy. He's my good baby. There's no dog in the world like Pookey. Honestly, if you would've come to me first, we could've come up with a better plan. But don't worry, you'll still get your cut.

SISSY: My what?

WAYNE: Your cut. Of the money.

SISSY: What money?

WAYNE: Oh, c'mon now. You knew about the insurance policy.

SISSY: Yes I did. That's why I sat down with her and wrote a letter that cancelled it.

WAYNE: But you didn't send it.

SISSY: No, you didn't send it. She gave it to you.

WAYNE: Why didn't you send it yourself, though? You could have. If you loved her so much.

SISSY: We just put the letter in an envelope and my client came. We needed a stamp and she had stamps at home. She was determined to use her stamp of Betty Boop. Sitting on a moon. In a bikini. With stripes and stars and the moon was yellow. I heard the story of the stamp a hundred and one times while my client was waiting. I had to get her out of there. I wasn't thinking.

WAYNE: Or maybe you were.

SISSY: I was gonna make sure she sent it!

WAYNE: Isn't it interesting? What we tell ourselves.

SISSY: It doesn't matter. They investigate these things. You won't have two pennies in your pockets when I'm finished with you.

WAYNE: I'd be careful if I were you.

SISSY: You'd be a lot of things if you were me. You wouldn't be wearing underwear with a lot of tongues hanging out of mouths.

WAYNE: Before you bring out your inner bitch, you might wanna think about what you did. Objectively, right? You entered my home. Without my permission. Got June in there. With a hundred and twenty pound dog. Made sure she couldn't escape.

SISSY: No, I locked myself out. Your dog came toward us barking. That's the reaction. You run.

WAYNE: If you can.

SISSY: I never would have taken her there if I knew you were keeping a dog killer in your basement!

WAYNE: POOKEY IS INNOCENT! HE WAS JUST PROTECTING HIS TERRITORY! THAT'S WHAT

DOGS DO! YOU'RE RESPONSIBLE FOR HER DEATH. THAT'S WHY YOU FEEL SO GUILTY.

SISSY: You need to leave now. Asshole.

WAYNE: What did you call me? *(He charges* SISSY.*)*

SISSY: Aaaaaaaah!

WAYNE: I didn't mean to scare you, but what's with the name-calling? People deserve more respect than that.

SISSY: I'm sorry.

WAYNE: You think you're better than everyone. What makes you better?

SISSY: Nothing. I don't think I am.

WAYNE: You're not even pretty. See, that's a nice way of saying it. I'm considering your feelings. I could've said you're an ugly, washed-up cum bucket, but I didn't.

SISSY: Thank you so much.

WAYNE: You don't have to thank me. It's just who I am. I see myself in other people. I see myself in you. I know what it's like to be in trouble. You don't realize. I'm the only one who can help you. All I have to do is tell the cops June had a key. She knew about the dog. She went where she didn't belong, and got what was coming. *(Pause)* But when the insurance folks come knocking on your door, you have to tell them the truth: June had no intention of cancelling that policy. She loved me like a son. I took over helping her with everything after Tom died. If you say anything that puts my inheritance in question, I'll chirp like a fucking chickadee, and you can kiss your life goodbye. We clear?

SISSY: Yes.

WAYNE: That's a good neighbor.

END OF PLAY